Up in the trees

A lot happens up in trees.
Trees are the habitat for
different living things.

Can you think of some living things that inhabit trees?

Some living things need
trees for shelter and for food.

Trees can offer food
such as seeds, twigs,
nuts, buds and bark.

Some living things have
adapted well to being high
up. A strong tail helps them
hang in the trees.

Gibbons have long arms so they can swing from tree to tree. They grab on with long fingers.

Some critters are green
or brown, like the trees
they are on! This helps to
keep them from harm.

You might have to strain your sight to see them! Can you spot an owl and a tree frog?

Tent caterpillars

Ants

Red bugs

You can see lots of insects creeping in and on trees. Bats, frogs and lizards feed on them.

High up in the crown of a
tree is a good spot for bees.

Trees are good for nests too.
The eggs are laid in the nest.
The chicks crack the eggshell
and push out.

Trees can be perfect
for sleeping as well.

Trees are fun for us too!
It is fun to be in a hut
high in a tree.

Zipping from tree to tree is good fun. You can get a burst of speed!

We can hang from trees too
– just like a gibbon can!

Words to blend

different	twigs	strong
helps	swing	from
grab	critters	frog
tent	ants	insects
spot	nests	crack
perfect	just	lizard
bees	shelter	harm

Before reading

Synopsis: Many animals and birds live in trees. The trees provide them with a safe habitat, food and shelter.

Review graphemes/phonemes: ee ow ai ur

Book discussion: Look at the cover and read the title together. Ask: *What kinds of animals and birds might you find living in trees? What do you think we will learn when we read this book?*

Link to prior learning: Display a word with adjacent consonants from the story, e.g. *sleeping.* Ask children to put a dot under each single-letter grapheme (*s, l, p, i*) and a line under the digraphs (*ee, ng*). Model, if necessary, how to sound out and blend the sounds together to read the word. Repeat with another word from the story, e.g. *strain,* and encourage children to sound out and blend the word independently.

Vocabulary check: habitat – a natural place to live in; critters – a slang word for animals

Decoding practice: Turn to page 15 and see how quickly children can find and read the word *speed.* Can they find another word with /ee/ on the page too? (*tree*)

Tricky word practice: Display the word *being* and ask children to circle the tricky part of the word (*e*, which makes the /ee/ sound). Practise writing and reading this word.

After reading

Apply learning: Ask: *Which animals in this book did you find most interesting? Why?*

Comprehension

- Can you name a creature that can hide in the tree where it lives?

- Can you name an animal that can hang from the trees?

- Where in a tree might you find a hive of bees?

Fluency

- Pick a page that most of the group read quite easily. Ask them to reread it with pace and expression. Model how to do this if necessary.

- Children could choose a favourite page to read aloud. Can they make their reading sound natural and fluent?

- Practise reading the words on page 17.

Tricky words review

the	are	you
some	have	to
being	so	they
your	out	be
we	like	push